Table of Contents

1020 Positive

Daily Affirmations for Black Women

By

Ella Greenfield

Introduction

Welcome to your transformative journey with "1020 Positive Daily Affirmations for Black Women," a sanctuary where words become the building blocks for a life filled with happiness, health, achievement, confidence, and self-love. This book is not just a collection of affirmations; it is a testament to black women's enduring spirit and resilience. Each affirmation is a breath of empowerment, a step towards embracing your fullest potential.

In these pages, you will find words that resonate with the core of your being. Crafted with love and intention, these affirmations are designed to uplift, inspire, and fortify you as you navigate the complexities of everyday life. From fostering mental wellness and physical health to igniting the flames of achievement and self-love, every affirmation is a beacon of strength, encouraging you to rise above challenges and celebrate your innate greatness.

This book is your daily companion, a source of strength in moments of doubt, and a celebratory shout in times of triumph. As you immerse yourself in these affirmations, you will begin to see a transformation in how you perceive yourself and interact with the world. These powerful statements will help you cultivate a mindset that not only dreams of success and happiness but actively manifests it.

Embrace each day with a heart full of courage and an unwavering belief in your worth. Let "1020 Positive Daily Affirmations for Black Women" guide you through self-discovery and empowerment, where every affirmation you speak is a step towards realizing the life you deserve.

Positive Affirmations for Black Women

I am worthy of receiving love, achieving success, and experiencing happiness.

Others find inspiration in my resilience.

I celebrate my distinctive beauty and glow.

I am an alchemist of positivity, transforming challenges into opportunities for growth and showcasing the enduring strength of black women.

I preserve our heritage, sharing the stories and traditions that highlight the rich legacy of black women.

I navigate change with resilience, adapting to life's dynamics with the fluid strength that black women embody.

I am a harmonious force, aligning with life's rhythms and amplifying the contributions of black women in arts, music, and culture.

I radiate love and kindness, enhancing the nurturing spirit within the black community.

I sculpt my destiny with purpose, demonstrating the determination and agency that characterize black women.

I authentically conduct the orchestra of my life, reflecting the vibrant voices of black women.

I cultivate joy, creating a celebratory atmosphere that mirrors the joyful spirit of being a black woman.

I strive for excellence, pushing myself to achieve greatness in all my endeavors.

I safeguard resilience, honoring the stories of black women who have triumphed over adversity.

I build dreams, creating a prosperous future with opportunities that honor the aspirations of black women.

I shine brightly, reflecting the inner brilliance and luminosity of black women.

I nurture sisterhood, strengthening the bonds within the black community.

I orchestrate empowerment, leading initiatives that uplift black women worldwide.

I draw wisdom from our history, embracing the insights passed down through generations.

I intertwine my aspirations with the collective dreams of black women, weaving a tapestry of shared goals and ambitions.

I achieve success with ease.

I actively shape my future.

I rightfully own abundance, and I accept it without hesitation.

I spread positivity and light wherever I go.

Being confident is intuitive to me.

Thanks to my life's wisdom, I possess unwavering clarity, making precise decisions.

Peace comes to me naturally as I cultivate tranquility within and around me.

My joy is contagious, enhancing the mood of my community and supporting fellow black women.

My mind is a wellspring of novel ideas that mirror the depth of black culture.

I ensure my actions are intentional, creating outcomes that reflect the aspirations of black women.

I actively maintain a positive environment that resonates with my community's energy.

I strive for and maintain balance, reflecting the enduring spirit of black women.

I appreciate every aspect of my journey, seeing value in all experiences.

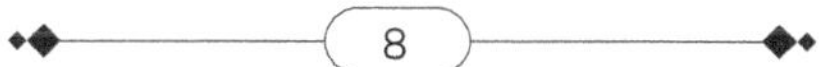

I effortlessly draw success, embracing achievements that highlight black women's excellence.

I confront fears with courage, inspired by the trailblazing black women before me.

I inspire myself and others by celebrating our collective historical achievements.

I welcome prosperity in its many forms, showcasing the rich contributions of black women.

I prioritize my overall health, valuing the narrative of self-care within the black community.

I contribute to shaping a more inclusive world that values black women's unique perspectives.

I fully accept my authentic self, enriching the narrative of black women.

I enhance my strength and that of others, tapping into our inherent potential.

I foster deep, meaningful relationships that celebrate community diversity.

I practice self-kindness, which is vital to my self-love journey.

Every experience enriches me with knowledge.

I continuously evolve, inspired by my community's ongoing development.

I fervently protect my aspirations, mirroring the tenacity of visionary black women.

I cultivate peace, maintaining calm during uncertain times.

I exude positivity, enhancing the collective mood and energy.

I initiate and inspire creativity, celebrating black artistic diversity.

I seize opportunities that align with my ambitions, embracing the limitless potential offered.

I value and affirm my worth, supporting a black women's empowerment narrative.

I offer consistent support to others, reinforcing our communal bonds.

I protect my personal space, ensuring my boundaries are respected.

I infuse my days with joy and laughter.

I honor the vibrant essence of being a black woman.

My resilience knows no bounds; I am unbreakable.

My life path demonstrates my unwavering strength.

I draw prosperity to all aspects of my life.

Love and joy are a constant presence in my life.

Self-love is essential to my well-being.

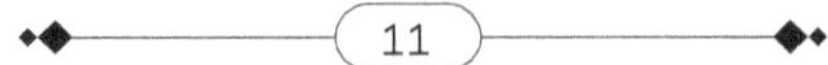

I am receptive to all of life's blessings.

Wealth and success come to me naturally.

Each step I take leads me closer to my grand aspirations.

My presence uplifts any environment.

I exude confidence, grace, and poise.

I acknowledge and utilize the magic within me.

Success and wealth are naturally attracted to me.

I foster a mindset of positivity.

I let go of my doubts and fully stepped into my power.

I spread love and kindness effortlessly.

Life's blessings are mine to claim.

I shape my joy.

I am confident in my ability to realize my ambitions.

I exhibit elegance and sophistication, representing the strength of black women.

I welcome an abundance that matches the resilience of black women.

I cherish and promote our rich cultural heritage.

I build unity and understanding in my community, strengthening our collective bonds.

I face challenges with unyielding courage, inspired by the boldness of past generations.

I envision a future filled with opportunities for black women.

My life is a resilient symphony, reflecting the enduring spirit of black women.

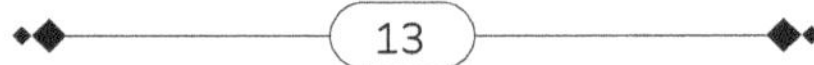

I constantly explore and embrace who I am as a black woman.

I express my unique style, contributing to the vibrant expressions of black women.

I turn challenges into growth opportunities, demonstrating black women's strength.

I preserve and celebrate our heritage, keeping the legacy of black women vibrant.

I adapt to changes with resilience, embodying the dynamic strength of black women.

I resonate with life's rhythms, echoing the cultural contributions of black women.

I am a source of love and compassion, nurturing the supportive spirit within our community.

I intentionally shape my destiny, driven by the determination of black women.

I lead my life authentically, representing the diverse voices of black women.

I strive for excellence in all my endeavors, aiming for greatness.

I preserve the stories of resilient black women, ensuring their legacies endure.

I embody elegance, showcasing my unique style and flair, adding to the rich mosaic of fashion and expression among black women.

I transform challenges into opportunities for growth, showcasing the strength inherent in black women.

I preserve and share black women's rich stories and traditions, safeguarding our legacy.

I adapt to life's changes with resilience and flexibility, reflecting the dynamic strength of black women.

I resonate with life's rhythms, amplifying the contributions of black women to art, music, and culture.

I radiate love and kindness, enhancing the supportive spirit within the black community.

I shape my destiny with deliberate intentions, channeling the determination of black women.

I lead my life authentically, representing black women's varied and vibrant voices.

I foster an atmosphere of celebration and happiness, embracing the joy that defines being a black woman.

I strive consistently for excellence in all my endeavors.

I preserve the stories of resilient black women, passing down their legacies of triumph.

I design a prosperous future with opportunities that honor the aspirations of black women.

I shine brightly, reflecting the brilliance and luminosity of black women.

I strengthen the bonds within the black community, enhancing our collective support and strength.

I drive initiatives that uplift and empower black women worldwide.

I gather wisdom from our collective experiences, sharing insights that span generations.

I intertwine my dreams with those of the collective, crafting a shared vision for the future.

I am a work of art in progress, continuously filled with love, joy, and abundance.

I am surrounded by people who uplift and support me.

I catalyze positive change, attracting opportunities for success.

I open my heart to both give and receive love freely.

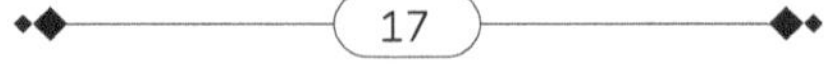

I embody resilience and power, limitless in my potential.

I inspire others, encouraging them to pursue their dreams.

I take pride in my growth and confidently radiate grace in every setting.

I naturally attract success and prosperity.

I maintain a positive mindset, attracting beneficial energies.

I shape my future, embracing love, success, and happiness as constant companions.

I accept and celebrate my uniqueness, which strengthens my confidence daily.

I magnetically draw abundance, fully deserving of all life has to offer.

I navigate life with faith, even in moments of uncertainty.

My spirit is indestructible.

I naturally repel negativity and attract positive outcomes.

I believe in the miracles life offers and welcome them with open arms.

I fully accept myself, releasing all doubts.

Achieving success is inherent to me.

I inspire others to embrace their dreams and follow their passions.

Love and abundance are always around me.

I trust my abilities to meet my goals.

Love flows freely to and from me.

I spread light and positivity wherever I go.

I fully deserve success and its rewards.

Every challenge is a stepping stone for growth.

I am an active creator of my desired reality.

I connect with those who share my vision and values.

My love for myself empowers me to live a fulfilling life.

I am resilient and competent in overcoming any challenge.

Gratitude fills me as I acknowledge the abundance in my life.

I author my own successful story.

My life is a continuous artwork, constantly evolving.

Opportunities that match my purpose find their way to me.

I am a beacon of love and positivity.

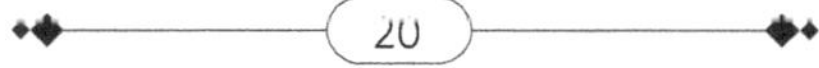

My life is abundant with love, joy, and prosperity.

I deserve all the beautiful things life offers.

I confidently create the life I desire.

I am a catalyst for positive change in the world.

Prosperity and success are my natural states.

Positive thoughts continuously fill my mind.

I am resilient, powerful, and limitless in my potential.

I take pride in my evolution.

I exude confidence and grace under all circumstances.

Prosperity flows through me.

My heart is always open to love.

I determine my destiny, accompanying love, success, and happiness.

I cherish my imperfections, which highlight my uniqueness.

Each day, my confidence grows stronger.

I am a magnet for abundance, attracting good effortlessly.

I trust my life's path, even in uncertainty.

My spirit is unshakable.

I choose positivity over negativity in all situations.

I am open to the miracles life presents.

I release all doubts and fully embrace my true self.

Success comes naturally to me.

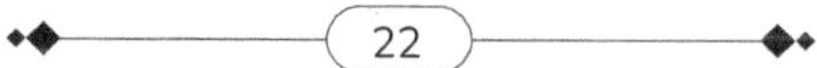

I inspire others to chase their goals with confidence.

My life is surrounded by love and prosperity.

I am confident in my abilities to achieve my goals.

My heart is open to love without reservation.

I illuminate the world with positivity.

I rightfully deserve success and all its benefits.

Each challenge I face is an opportunity for personal growth.

I am a powerful creator of my life's narrative.

I draw like-minded individuals to me.

My self-love enables me to create a joyful and fulfilling life.

I am resilient and ready to overcome any obstacles.

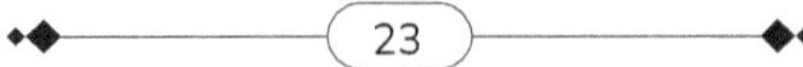

I am grateful for the constant flow of abundance into my life.

I am the author of my success story.

My life is a masterpiece, continuously evolving.

I attract opportunities that align with my life's purpose.

I am a beacon of love and positivity.

My life journey is enriched with love, joy, and abundance.

I deserve the best that life has to offer.

I trust in my ability to manifest the life I desire.

I am a force for positive change.

Success and prosperity are my natural states.

My thoughts are consistently positive.

I am resilient and powerful.

My potential knows no bounds.

I am proud of who I am becoming.

I maintain confidence and grace in every situation.

Prosperity and success continuously flow through me.

My heart is always open to love.

I take charge of my destiny.

Love, success, and happiness are my constant companions.

I value my unique traits, which make me special.

My confidence increases with each passing day.

Abundance naturally gravitates towards me.

I am worthy of all life's blessings.

I have faith in my journey, even when it's unclear.

My spirit is invincible.

I attract positive outcomes and repel negativity.

I am a magnet for life's wonders.

I let go of all my doubts and entirely accepted myself.

Success is my inherent state.

I inspire others to follow their dreams.

I am enveloped by love and abundance.

I trust my capability to meet my objectives.

My heart freely gives and receives love.

I spread light and positivity everywhere I go.

I fully deserve success and its rewards.

Every obstacle I encounter is an opportunity for growth.

I am an active creator of my desired reality.

I connect with individuals who share my positive outlook.

My self-love empowers me to live a fulfilling life.

I am resilient and able to surmount any challenge.

I am thankful for the abundance flowing into my life.

I am the narrator of my success story.

My life is a continuously evolving masterpiece.

I draw opportunities that resonate with my goals.

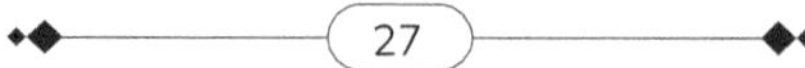

I am a beacon of love and positivity.

I attract positive change, fostering a world that values diversity and inclusion.

I advocate for the recognition and visibility of black women, championing their representation.

I draw upon the resilience of those before me, embodying their wisdom.

I use my voice to highlight and elevate the experiences of black women.

I celebrate and honor the diversity of black beauty, creating beauty in my recognition.

I inspire black women to embrace and love their natural selves.

I navigate life's challenges with the inherent grace and power of black women.

I draw uplifting and positive energy towards myself, resonating

with my spirit.

I prioritize nurturing my mind, body, and soul and understanding the importance of self-care.

I gracefully overcome challenges, fortified by inherent strength.

I make clear and aligned decisions that serve my best interests.

I cultivate relationships with uplifting individuals, enhancing my life.

I carefully select my thoughts, fostering a mindset that uplifts and empowers me.

I find joy in life's simple pleasures, creating laughter and happiness.

I embrace personal growth, seizing opportunities to develop.

I effortlessly attract positive energy, filling my life with good vibes.

I recover from setbacks with resilience, demonstrating grace and strength.

I motivate myself and others to keep going, even against the odds.

I build harmonious relationships, nurturing understanding and connection.

I carefully nurture my dreams, dedicating myself to their realization.

I confidently express my creativity, trusting in my unique ideas.

I explore new aspects of myself daily, embarking on a journey of self-discovery.

I embrace challenges with courage, stepping boldly into new experiences.

I appreciate the abundance around me and maintain a grateful heart.

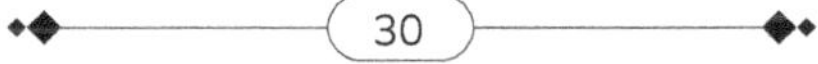

I inspire self-belief in myself and others, empowering those around me.

I constantly evolve, always moving towards the best version of myself.

I wisely use my time, investing it in pursuits that align with my aspirations.

I acknowledge the wealth of opportunities before me, creating abundance.

I live mindfully, fully present in each moment.

I extend kindness to myself and others, nurturing compassion.

I trust in my life's journey, confident in its unfolding.

I cultivate deep, meaningful relationships enriched by love.

I inspire creativity and passion in those I meet, igniting their potential.

I maintain a positive outlook, choosing optimism in all circumstances.

I balance my life, harmonizing my physical, mental, and spiritual well-being.

I live authentically, fully embracing my true self.

I continually learn from each experience, attracting wisdom.

I find inner peace, maintaining calm within myself and my environment.

I spread joy, brightening the world with my presence.

I uplift others, recognizing their strength and potential.

I prioritize my well-being, integrating self-care into my daily routine.

I make a positive impact, improving the well-being of others.

I embrace success, welcoming achievements with joy.

I reflect inwardly, growing and evolving from my experiences.

I foster hope and resilience, inspiring those I meet with optimism.

I practice self-compassion, treating myself with kindness and understanding.

I attract prosperity in all areas of my life, welcoming abundance.

I inspire others to reach for their potential, empowering them to succeed.

I overcome obstacles with steadfast resilience, demonstrating my strength.

I invest my energy wisely, focusing on positive pursuits.

I establish beneficial habits that support my overall well-being.

I find serenity amid life's ups and downs, maintaining peace.

I prioritize activities that nurture my soul, understanding the value of self-care.

I express gratitude for all experiences, appreciating life's full spectrum.

I embrace my authentic self, loving and accepting who I am.

I ignite creativity in others, inspiring them through my actions.

I recognize the extraordinary in everyday life, attracting miracles.

I protect my inner peace, setting boundaries that maintain my tranquility.

I contribute to a kinder world, fostering positive change.

I share my thoughts and feelings openly, advocating for authentic self-expression.

I learn and grow from every experience, filled with wisdom.

I extend compassion universally, radiating love to all beings.

I encourage others to follow their dreams, supporting their aspirations.

I achieve my goals with focus and determination, succeeding in my endeavors.

I nurture my dreams with passion, dedicated to their fulfillment.

I find happiness in the journey and the destination, celebrating life's joys.

I balance various aspects of my life, maintaining harmony.

I inspire optimism and resilience, bringing hope to those around me.

I spread kindness wherever I go, enhancing the lives of others.

I honor my cultural heritage, enriching my life with its richness.

I pursue my aspirations with the tenacity of a queen, resilient and determined.

I delight in the vibrancy of black culture, finding joy in its beauty.

I support fellow black women, encouraging their endeavors and successes.

I break barriers and achieve greatness, redefining success on my terms.

I confidently embrace my identity as a black woman, empowered by my grace and power.

I live authentically, true to my roots and values.

I create inclusive spaces that uplift and celebrate black women.

I draw from the resilience of the black community, strengthened by our shared stories of triumph.

I cultivate self-love, recognizing the beauty in every shade of melanin.

I use my influence to uplift and empower black women, promoting positive change.

I surround myself with relationships that respect and honor my true essence.

I inspire black women to embrace their unique journeys, recognizing their limitless potential.

I advocate for fearless self-expression, proudly showcasing my identity as a black woman.

I have the wisdom and strength of my ancestors, fortified by their enduring spirit.

I preserve and celebrate my cultural heritage, cherishing the traditions that define me.

I infuse every interaction with love and light, creating positive energy.

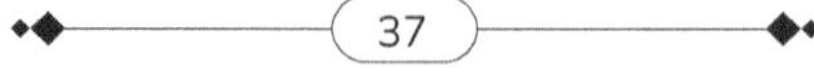

I face challenges with the resilience typical of black women, who are unyielding.

I celebrate my melanin, recognizing the beauty within myself.

I encourage black women to recognize and utilize their unique talents and gifts.

I foster sisterhood, building connections and support within the black community.

I appreciate the richness and diversity of black heritage, celebrating our cultural contributions.

I actively contribute to breaking down barriers and promoting equality, championing positive change.

I express the various facets of my identity as a black woman, embracing my complexity.

I draw inspiration from the resilience of black women who have paved the way.

I stand proud in my blackness, confident in my beauty and abilities.

I uplift fellow black women, helping them overcome obstacles and achieve their goals.

I attract opportunities that showcase and honor the brilliance of black women.

I chart my course with the knowledge of my limitless potential.

I contribute to narratives highlighting black women's successes, amplifying our achievements.

I remind black women of their worth and capabilities, empowering them to succeed.

I embrace and express the unique facets of being a black woman and living authentically.

I share and celebrate the traditions that shape my identity and am proud of my cultural pride.

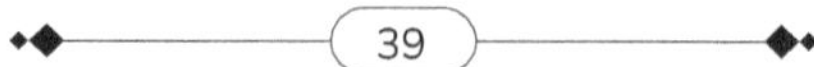

I navigate life's challenges with the resilience inherited from generations of black women.

I cultivate spaces that foster love, respect, and understanding for black women.

I encourage black women to dream big and pursue their aspirations with zeal.

I leave a legacy that uplifts and inspires future generations, making a positive impact.

I support the ambitions of black women, encouraging them to reach for their dreams.

I advocate for self-love, recognizing its transformative power.

I help other black women see their strengths and potential, empowering them to excel.

I inspire creativity, innovation, and excellence within the black community, fostering unity.

I build solidarity among black women, strengthening our collective bonds.

I honor the achievements of black women, preserving their legacy.

I celebrate my identity, finding joy in being a black woman.

I remind black women they are supported in their journey, fostering a sense of community.

I express my unique voice and perspective as a black woman, sharing my story.

I tap into black women's collective wisdom and resilience, drawing strength from our shared experiences.

I exude confidence, pride in my abilities, and self-assurance.

I attract good vibes effortlessly, filled with positive energy.

I recover from challenges with grace, demonstrating resilience and strength.

I motivate myself and others to continue striving, nurturing our perseverance.

I foster understanding and connection, building harmonious relationships.

I nurture my dreams with dedication and am committed to their realization.

I express my creativity with confidence, trusting in my unique ideas.

I explore new aspects of myself each day on a continuous journey of self-discovery.

I approach new challenges with courage, ready to face the unknown.

I remain grateful for the abundance in my life, appreciating all I have.

I empower myself and others to believe in our potential, inspiring self-confidence.

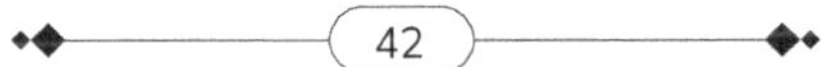

I embrace positive transformations, constantly evolving to become my best self.

I invest my time wisely, focusing on goals that align with my values.

I recognize the abundance of opportunities around me, seizing them with enthusiasm.

I savor each moment, living mindfully and with presence.

I extend kindness to myself and others, nurturing a compassionate spirit.

I trust in the process of my life, confident in its joyous unfolding.

I deepen my connections, fostering love and meaningful relationships.

I ignite passion and creativity in those I meet, inspiring them to embrace their potential.

I choose optimism in every situation, maintaining a positive outlook.

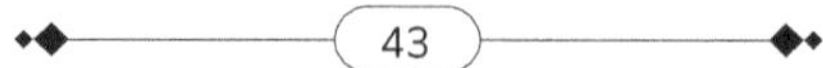

I maintain balance, harmonizing my physical, mental, and spiritual well-being.

I live true to myself, authentically embracing who I am.

I learn from each experience, gathering wisdom along the way.

I find peace within myself and my environment, cultivating a serene atmosphere.

I spread happiness, brightening the world with my joyous presence.

I uplift others, helping them recognize their inner strength.

I prioritize my health and well-being, integrating self-care into my daily routine.

I positively impact others, improving their well-being through my actions.

I embrace achievements with open arms, celebrating success.

I grow from within, reflecting and evolving through self-reflection.

I inspire hope and resilience, bringing optimism to those I meet.

I gracefully navigate life's challenges, fortified by determination and clarity.

I make decisions that reflect my true desires, aligning with my highest good.

I draw uplifting connections, surrounding myself with positive individuals.

I safeguard my mindset, fostering thoughts that strengthen and empower me.

I discover joy in life's simple moments, creating laughter everywhere.

I embrace personal growth, seizing every opportunity to develop further.

I practice self-compassion, treating myself with kindness and understanding.

I attract prosperity, welcoming abundance into every aspect of my life.

I inspire others to realize their potential, serving as a beacon of empowerment.

I overcome challenges with steadfast resilience, showcasing my inner strength.

I celebrate the diversity within the black community, empowering its unique voices.

I fill my life with love, light, and positivity, attracting positive energy effortlessly.

I embrace my unique voice and perspective, guarding my self-expression.

I blend traditions and innovations, creating a cultural fusion that honors my heritage.

I stand resilient against challenges, embodying the strength of black women.

I foster a supportive community where black women uplift one another.

I live authentically, showing the many facets of my identity without apology.

I inspire black women to acknowledge and embrace their power.

I achieve greatness and break barriers, attracting success in my endeavors.

I nurture a profound love for myself, celebrating my uniqueness.

I share stories that highlight the resilience and triumphs of black women.

I remind black women that their dreams are both valid and achievable.

I work to create inclusive spaces that celebrate diversity.

I access ancestral wisdom, serving as a beacon of knowledge.

I build unity and sisterhood among black women across the globe.

I carve my path with intention and clarity, guarding my self-determination.

I find happiness in black culture's beauty and richness, creating joy in my life.

I encourage black women to use their voices for positive change.

I express my identity boldly and without apology, championing self-expression.

I embody the resilience of black women who have faced and overcome adversity.

I spread love and compassion to myself and those around me.

I contribute to societal change, actively dismantling barriers and promoting equality.

I nurture black women's dreams, helping them flourish and succeed.

I cultivate an environment that respects and honors diverse backgrounds.

I uplift black women, encouraging them to shine in their brilliance.

I confidently express my true self, championing authenticity.

I wisely invest my energy in positive and fulfilling endeavors.

I create habits that enhance my well-being, supporting a healthy lifestyle.

I prioritize activities that nourish my soul, emphasizing the importance of self-care.

I express gratitude for both challenges and victories,

maintaining a thankful spirit.

I accept my true self with love and embrace authenticity fully.

I ignite creativity in others, inspiring them with my actions.

I recognize the extraordinary in everyday life, welcoming miracles.

I protect my inner peace, setting boundaries to maintain tranquility.

I drive positive change, contributing to a kinder, more inclusive world.

I share my thoughts and feelings openly, valuing authentic self-expression.

I grow and learn from every experience, embodying wisdom.

I extend compassion to all, radiating love and kindness.

I motivate others to pursue their dreams with passion and determination.

I focus on achieving my goals with unwavering focus and determination.

I nurture my dreams with dedication, committing to their realization.

I balance various aspects of my life, seeking harmony and equilibrium.

I inspire optimism and resilience in those around me, fostering hope.

I spread kindness wherever I go, enhancing the lives of others.

I acknowledge my strength and empower myself continuously.

I open my heart to opportunities, attracting them with positivity.

I honor and protect my well-being by maintaining healthy boundaries.

I appreciate beauty in all forms, recognizing elegance in simplicity and complexity.

I persist through challenges, demonstrating perseverance.

I accept all parts of myself without judgment, practicing acceptance.

I make wise choices aligned with my higher self and guided by wisdom.

I motivate others, sparking their drive and ambition.

I nourish my body, mind, and spirit, attracting vibrant health.

I focus my attention on what truly matters, maintaining clarity and purpose.

I uplift the energy around me, creating positive vibrations.

I extend kindness to myself and others, nurturing compassion.

I cultivate happiness in my life, fostering joyous environments.

I trust my capabilities, embrace my uniqueness, and am confident in my journey.

I encourage growth and support in others, creating a nurturing atmosphere.

I welcome prosperity and success, attracting them effortlessly.

I passionately pursue my dreams with dedication and enthusiasm.

I promote harmony within and around me, fostering peace.

I appreciate my worth, celebrating self-love.

I express gratitude for the abundance in my life and thankful for my blessings.

I empower myself and others, contributing to the collective strength of black women.

I inspire creativity and passion in fellow black women, fostering innovation.

I build connections that strengthen the black community, promoting unity.

I draw strength from the stories of resilient black women motivated by their legacy.

I make a lasting impact, inspiring future generations with positive contributions.

I support black women in realizing their unique potential and achieving their dreams.

I love myself unconditionally, recognizing and celebrating my divine beauty with pride.

I help black women see their value, assisting them on their empowerment journey.

I lead by example, breaking barriers and setting a path for future generations of black women.

I advocate boldly for self-expression, sharing the unique aspects of my identity with courage and authenticity.

I realize my success enhances the collective strength and empowerment of black women.

I inspire other black women to pursue their interests and live truthfully and passionately.

I cultivate a sense of sisterhood and cooperative spirit within the black community.

I support black women dreaming ambitiously and pursuing their objectives with unwavering resolve.

I celebrate the diversity and richness of black cultures across the globe, fostering cultural appreciation.

I uplift black women to meet challenges and excel in all life's aspects.

I wholeheartedly embrace my unique beauty and inspire others to do the same, promoting self-love.

I leverage my influence to fight for justice, equality, and positive transformation.

I stand resilient against societal challenges and stereotypes, embodying strength.

I build and strengthen community ties to uplift the black community.

I preserve and relay the impactful stories of black women who have historically shaped our journey.

I inject joy, laughter, and vibrancy into my life and the lives of those around me.

I encourage black women to pursue their dreams and ambitions fearlessly.

I commit to continuous self-discovery, deepening my understanding of my identity.

I motivate black women to unleash their creativity and showcase their unique talents.

I promote love and unity within the black community and extend it outward.

I contribute to the progress that specifically aids black women in moving forward.

I draw strength from the enduring legacy of black women pioneers, fortifying my resilience.

I create bridges between diverse black cultures, celebrating our interconnectedness and shared heritage.

I remind black women of their transformative power and intrinsic strength.

I foster an environment where every black woman can feel loved and appreciated for her true self.

I strive to lift others as I advance, ensuring collective elevation.

I light the way for the next generations of black women, offering guidance and inspiration.

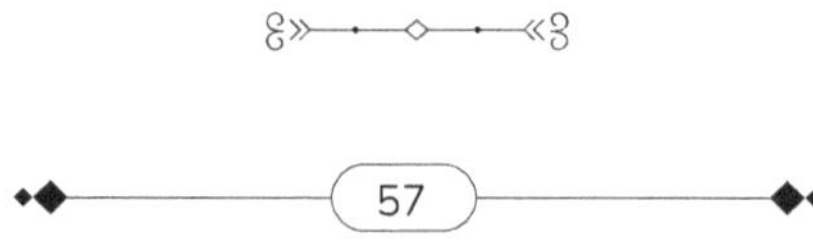

I encourage collaboration that enhances the collective power and impact of black women.

I motivate black women to follow their passions with dedication and enthusiasm.

I weave together the varied threads of black cultures, creating a tapestry that celebrates our collective beauty.

I empower black women to overcome obstacles and excel in every endeavor.

I emphasize the power of our voices and the uniqueness of our stories, championing self-expression.

I underline the importance of mutual support and uplift within our community.

I stand steadfast against adversity, inspiring others with my resilience.

I actively engage in efforts to dismantle systemic inequalities, promoting positive change.

I safeguard and cherish the rich traditions of black culture, ensuring they are honored and passed down.

I revel in celebrating black achievements and excellence, finding joy in our successes.

I inspire black women to pursue education and personal growth, expanding their horizons.

I affirm that my value transcends societal expectations, promoting self-worth.

I use my abilities to inspire and elevate those around me, contributing to our collective empowerment.

I spark creativity and innovation within the black community, encouraging new ideas and perspectives.

I attract unity, building strong connections that fortify the black community.

I channel the resilience of black women who have faced adversity, fortifying my strength.

I am thankful for each moment and the blessings it brings.

I attract successful outcomes with ease.

I choose joy in every situation, safeguarding my happiness.

I develop habits that nurture my health and well-being.

I persist through challenges with steadfast strength, embodying resilience.

I extend kindness and compassion in all my interactions.

I am committed to personal growth, continually evolving into a better version of myself.

I draw prosperity to all facets of my life, thriving in abundance.

I spread positivity, impacting those around me with good vibes.

I wisely use my time, focusing on goals that matter.

I see and celebrate beauty everywhere, enhancing my appreciation of the world.

I inspire others to recognize and embrace their unique qualities.

I draw supportive and uplifting relationships with myself.

I trust in my abilities and embrace my potential with confidence.

I generously share love, enriching my life and the lives of others.

I passionately pursue my dreams, dedicating myself to achieving them.

I initiate positive changes, contributing to a kinder world.

I uplift those in need of support, offering encouragement and guidance.

I recognize the magic in everyday moments, attracting miracles.

I live authentically, embracing my true self without compromise.

I learn from every experience, gaining wisdom as I go.

I confidently assert my uniqueness and capabilities.

I shine light and kindness, positively affecting my environment.

I form meaningful connections that enrich my soul.

I rebound from setbacks with increased strength and resilience.

I maintain balance in my life, gracefully managing various aspects.

I empower myself and others to achieve greatness.

I ignite creativity in those around me, sparking innovation.

I welcome good fortune and receiving life's blessings with gratitude.

I treat myself with tenderness and understanding, practicing self-compassion.

I align my thoughts with positive outcomes, focusing on growth.

I generate positive energy, uplifting every situation with optimism.

I drive myself towards ambitious goals with unwavering motivation.

I reach my objectives with determination and persistence.

I grow and adapt through each experience, continuously evolving.

I express gratitude daily, appreciating life's beauty.

I fearlessly embrace my true self, living authentically.

I attract abundance, flourishing in prosperity.

I prioritize my health and happiness, treating self-care as essential.

I discover joy in all experiences, celebrating life's diversity.

I support others with words of encouragement and actions of kindness.

I show unwavering kindness, nurturing myself and extending it to others.

I transform for the better, constantly evolving into the best version of myself.

I openly express my thoughts and feelings, sharing my voice with the world.

I confront challenges with courage and resilience.

I nurture my dreams with constant care and commitment.

I cultivate peace within, embracing tranquility in my inner world.

I empower myself, recognizing the immense strength within.

I give and receive love abundantly, enriching my life and those around me.

I inspire hope and faith, uplifting the spirits of others.

I balance my life's various elements, seeking harmony.

I honor and express my authenticity, valuing my true self.

I consistently choose optimism, maintaining a positive outlook.

I make clear decisions that reflect my true intentions.

I attract positive energy, enhancing the vibe wherever I go.

I access my inner strength, facing life's challenges confidently.

I am a champion for self-love, embracing myself with compassion and acceptance.

I am a source of empowerment, inspiring myself and others to thrive.

I am a guardian of my inner peace, cultivating tranquility within.

I am a creator of joy, finding delight in ordinary and extraordinary moments.

I am a magnet for clarity, discerning opportunities, and solutions.

I champion self-care, prioritizing activities that nourish my mind, body, and soul.

I am a vessel of gratitude, expressing thanks for life's journey and its lessons.

I am a beacon of inspiration, igniting creativity in those around me.

I am a source of empowerment, embracing and utilizing my power.

I am a magnet for positive energy, infusing optimism into every interaction.

I am a guardian of my potential, unlocking new possibilities with each step.

I create peace, spreading calm and tranquility throughout my surroundings.

I am a champion for resilience, rebounding from challenges with greater strength.

I create a positive impact, recognizing and celebrating black women's contributions.

I am a source of encouragement, affirming that the aspirations of black women are valid and achievable.

I am a champion for self-expression, fearlessly and authentically sharing the unique facets of my identity.

I am a vessel of empowerment, acknowledging that my achievements contribute to the collective strength of black women.

I am a beacon of inspiration, motivating black women to follow their passions and live authentically.

I am a magnet for unity, nurturing sisterhood, and collaboration within the black community.

I am a guardian of dreams, supporting black women to dream ambitiously and pursue their goals with tenacity.

I am a creator of cultural appreciation, celebrating the diversity and richness of black cultures globally.

I am a source of encouragement, uplifting black women to overcome challenges and excel in all aspects of life.

I champion self-love, encouraging others to embrace their unique beauty.

I am a vessel of empowerment, leveraging my influence to advocate for justice, equality, and positive change.

I am a beacon of strength, resiliently standing against societal challenges and stereotypes.

I am a magnet for community, fostering connections and collaboration that uplift the black community.

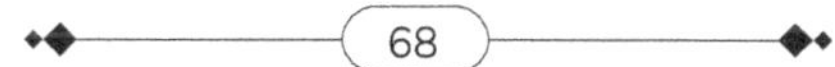

I am a guardian of history, preserving and sharing the influential stories of black women who have shaped history.

I am a creator of joy, infusing laughter, celebration, and vibrancy into every aspect of my life.

I am a source of encouragement, inspiring black women to embrace their ambitions boldly.

I am a champion for self-awareness, continuously exploring and understanding the depths of my identity.

I am a vessel of inspiration, encouraging black women to explore their originality and express their unique talents.

I am a beacon of love, promoting love and unity within the black community and extending it beyond.

I am a magnet for progress, actively contributing to advancements that benefit black women.

I am a guardian of resilience, drawing strength from the enduring legacy of black women who have blazed trails.

I am a creator of cultural fusion, bridging the gaps between diverse black cultures and celebrating their interconnectedness.

I am a beacon of strength, navigating challenges with grace and determination.

I am a source of compassion, extending understanding and empathy to myself and others.

I am a magnet for positive transformations, continually evolving into the best version of myself.

I empower myself and others, understanding that my achievements contribute significantly to the collective success of black women.

I inspire black women to pursue their dreams and authentically express their true selves passionately.

I enhance unity within the black community, promoting sisterhood and cooperative efforts.

I motivate black women to set ambitious goals and relentlessly chase them fervently.

I honor and celebrate the rich diversity of black cultures around the world.

I uplift black women, helping them navigate and triumph over their challenges.

I advocate for self-love, celebrating my beauty and encouraging others to appreciate themselves.

I embody strength, drawing resilience from the enduring spirit of my ancestors.

I rejoice in our cultural heritage, actively honoring the traditions that connect me to my roots.

I actively engage in initiatives that drive positive change and elevate black communities.

I am dedicated to continuous learning and sharing knowledge to enlighten and inspire future generations.

I create inclusive environments that value and respect the rich diversity within the black diaspora.

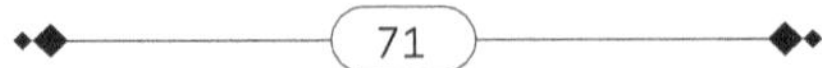

I energize those around me to follow their passions and realize their dreams without hesitation.

I assert my autonomy, embracing my journey as integral to the collective empowerment of black women.

I am genuine to myself, celebrating my individuality in a world that appreciates my uniqueness.

I spark innovation and creativity within the black community, encouraging artistic and intellectual expression.

I weave stronger bonds within the black community, enhancing our collective voice and impact.

I support black women in boldly and fearlessly pursuing their dreams.

I raise awareness about the rich tapestry of black experiences, fostering a deeper understanding and appreciation.

I offer constant encouragement, reinforcing the resilience that characterizes black women.

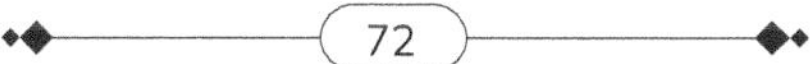

I promote self-love, affirming that true beauty is rooted in authenticity and self-acceptance.

§»——◇——«§

I lend my strength to uplift those needing support, amplifying our collective power through solidarity.

§»——◇——«§

I share wisdom, tapping into the community's vast knowledge to guide and educate.

§»——◇——«§

I attract joy and prosperity, enriching every aspect of my life with positivity and abundance.

§»——◇——«§

I express myself confidently, contributing my voice to the chorus of diverse black narratives.

§»——◇——«§

I empower through my actions and words, advocating for equality and justice in every sphere.

§»——◇——«§

I stand as a beacon of hope, guiding others towards a future where they can freely pursue their aspirations.

§»——◇——«§

I establish connections that enhance and strengthen the black community's fabric.

I draw from the resilience of black women who have historically overcome obstacles, using their stories to fortify my resolve.

I create impactful change, actively ensuring that black women's contributions are acknowledged and celebrated.

I encourage black women to own their stories and shine in their authentic light.

I champion self-love, knowing that recognizing my worth sets a powerful example for others.

I leverage my strengths to uplift the community, fostering a culture of empowerment and support.

I illuminate paths for others, demonstrating that pursuing one's passion is possible and essential.

I promote unity, helping to forge strong alliances that enhance collective resilience and impact.

I nurture the dreams of black women, encouraging them to envision and work towards expansive and bold futures.

I celebrate the myriad cultures within the black community, recognizing that our diversity is our strength.

I am a source of positive reinforcement, reminding black women of their innate power and potential.

I embrace every aspect of my identity, understanding that self-acceptance is a profound act of rebellion and empowerment.

I share resources and knowledge to uplift others, ensuring empowerment is a shared journey.

I radiate love and wisdom, creating an environment where others feel valued and inspired.

I engage actively in efforts that challenge inequalities, striving to make a lasting difference.

I preserve the narratives of black history, ensuring that the legacies of those who came before us continue to educate and inspire.

I bring joy into every space, celebrating the vibrancy and achievements of black culture.

I foster an atmosphere of support and encouragement, ensuring every black woman knows she is not alone in her endeavors.

I encourage introspection and self-discovery, recognizing that personal understanding enriches one's life and community.

I act as a conduit for creativity, encouraging black women to explore and express their innate talents.

I spread love throughout my community, believing unity and affection can transform society.

I contribute to progress by supporting initiatives that advance the well-being of black women.

I stand resilient, sharing the collective strength of black women who have navigated adversity.

I bridge cultural divides, celebrating the interconnectedness and shared experiences within the black community.

I encourage every black woman to stand firm and resilient, navigating challenges with grace and determination.

I extend compassion and understanding, fostering a nurturing environment where all can thrive.

I embrace transformation, continually evolving into the best version of myself and setting a positive example for others to follow.

I safeguard my energy, focusing on relationships and endeavors that bring positivity and growth.

I generate abundance, attracting prosperity to enrich my life and community.

I inspire through my actions and words, motivating others to believe in the power of their dreams.

I champion self-love, knowing that loving oneself revolutionizes how we interact with the world.

I maintain good health, understanding that a sound body and mind are foundational to achieving one's goals.

I give thanks continually, recognizing that gratitude magnifies life's blessings and fosters an optimistic outlook.

I uplift those needing encouragement, providing a supportive word or gesture to brighten their paths.

I pursue my dreams with relentless passion and resilience, setting an example of dedication and commitment.

I inject happiness into my daily life, finding joy in significant milestones and simple pleasures.

I foster positive relationships, surrounding myself with individuals who uplift and inspire.

I practice mindfulness, cherishing each moment and living fully present.

I seek wisdom in all experiences, valuing the lessons each one teaches.

I exude positivity, influencing my surroundings with a hopeful spirit.

I energize black women to pursue their dreams without hesitation and confidently.

I continuously explore and deepen my self-awareness, understanding every identity layer.

I inspire black women to unleash their creativity and proudly share their talents.

I promote love and unity, fostering a supportive atmosphere within and beyond the black community.

I actively participate in initiatives that drive progress and create opportunities for black women.

I derive strength from the enduring legacy of black women pioneers, bolstering my resilience.

I bridge cultural divides, celebrating the rich interconnectedness of diverse black cultures.

I reinforce the transformative power inherent in black women, encouraging them to harness it.

I fully accept all parts of myself with love, fostering self-acceptance in others.

I elevate others as I ascend, ensuring collective advancement within the black community.

I illuminate paths for future generations, setting an example of empowered living.

I strengthen the bonds of sisterhood in the black community through collaborative efforts.

I champion the pursuit of dreams with unwavering determination, supporting black women to aim high.

I weave a tapestry of appreciation for the diverse cultures within the black diaspora.

I back black women in their efforts to excel across all fields, offering support and motivation.

I celebrate the authenticity of my voice and encourage others to do the same.

I uplift and support my community, understanding the importance of our collective strength.

I remain steadfast in adversity, inspiring others with my resilience.

I actively contribute to dismantling systemic inequalities and advocating for fair and just treatment.

I preserve and honor the rich heritage of black traditions, passing down valuable cultural knowledge.

I create moments of joy, celebrating black excellence and achievements.

I motivate black women to pursue educational and personal growth opportunities.

I affirm the intrinsic value of self-love, challenging societal norms and expectations.

I leverage my influence to inspire and uplift those around me, spreading creativity and innovation.

I am true to myself, freely expressing my uniqueness and inspiring others to do the same.

I cultivate a peaceful inner world, ensuring tranquility follows me.

I rejoice in everyday joys, elevating my spirit and those around me.

I attract positivity effortlessly, becoming a beacon of good vibes.

I practice self-compassion, treating myself with kindness and encouraging others to do the same.

I confront challenges with courage, showing resilience in every test.

I am thankful for life's abundance, recognizing the gifts in big and small experiences.

I empower myself to overcome obstacles, acknowledging my inner strength.

I attract abundant love, enriching my life with deep, meaningful relationships.

I commit to pursuing my dreams with passion and persistence.

I cultivate serenity, ensuring peace surrounds me and influences my environment.

I reflect on my experiences, learning and evolving from each one.

I offer words of support to those in need, strengthening my community with kindness.

I attract nurturing relationships that contribute to my personal growth.

I am authentic in every expression, confidently showing the world my true self.

I acquire wisdom from life's lessons, growing more insightful each day.

I create significant change, contributing to a kinder, more compassionate world.

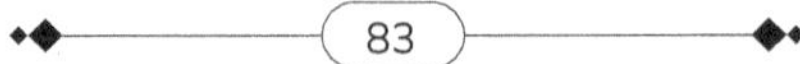

I care for my well-being, recognizing the importance of maintaining health.

I rebound from challenges with robust strength, demonstrating the resilience of black women.

I champion self-love, embracing my uniqueness and inspiring others to love themselves.

I transform continuously, constantly evolving into a better version of myself.

I balance my life's demands, finding harmony in my personal and professional life.

I give thanks regularly, appreciating every lesson and blessing.

I navigate life with confidence, facing each day with grace and strength.

I make clear, aligned decisions that reflect my best intentions.

I foster supportive connections, enriching my life and the lives of others.

I infuse purpose into all my actions, making meaningful contributions to my community.

I encourage positive interactions, ensuring that my relationships are uplifting and beneficial.

I unlock new possibilities, embracing each opportunity that comes my way.

I am grateful for every blessing and for recognizing the abundance flowing into my life.

I inspire creativity and passion, encouraging others to explore their unique potential.

I adapt with flexibility and strength, showing resilience in the face of change.

I radiate peace, creating calm amid life's hustle.

I attract success, aligning with opportunities that match my skills and ambitions.

I maintain a joyful outlook, finding happiness in a variety of situations.

I establish healthy habits that enhance my overall well-being.

I uplift others with supportive words, fostering a nurturing environment.

I accept all parts of myself with love, promoting holistic self-acceptance.

I confront life's challenges with bravery, embodying courage in every action.

I acquire knowledge from every experience, continually enriching my understanding.

I cultivate positive thoughts, ensuring my mindset supports my well-being.

I follow my dreams with determination, showing the power of focused ambition.

I create an atmosphere of love, spreading warmth and compassion to all around me.

I recognize my ability to overcome any challenge, tapping into the deep reservoir of strength within me.

I explore my true self, engaging in a journey of self-discovery that enlightens and enriches.

I invite abundance into my life, welcoming prosperity in all its forms.

I exhibit kindness without reservation, offering compassion to myself and extending it to others.

I find balance in all aspects of life, ensuring my actions reflect my values and needs.

I perceive opportunities clearly, making decisions that propel me forward.

I prioritize my health, understanding that a strong foundation supports all other endeavors.

I embrace authenticity, living in alignment with my true self and values.

I champion self-love, fully embracing my worth and celebrating my individuality.

I effortlessly attract positive energy, filling my life with good vibrations.

I am a beacon of resilience, gracefully overcoming obstacles and emerging stronger.

I create harmonious relationships, building understanding and connections.

I empower myself and others, encouraging the embrace of our collective strengths.

I vigilantly maintain my boundaries, ensuring they reflect my values and contribute to my well-being.

I express myself confidently, sharing my thoughts and ideas freely.

I draw meaningful connections to those who uplift and inspire me.

I embody resilience, facing life's challenges with grace and determination.

I make a meaningful difference, creating a positive impact in my environment.

I cultivate a powerful mindset, focusing on thoughts that empower and uplift.

I enjoy life's simple pleasures, embracing moments of laughter and happiness.

I seize growth opportunities, always striving to evolve and improve.

I treat myself with kindness and understanding, practicing self-compassion.

I attract abundance, welcoming prosperity across all areas of my life.

I inspire others to reach their full potential, lighting the path for them to thrive.

I overcome obstacles with unwavering strength, embodying resilience.

I choose to invest my energy in positive and enriching endeavors.

I strengthen the bonds within the black community, fostering unity and collaboration.

I draw strength from the inspiring stories of black women who have faced challenges head-on.

I contribute to a world that values and celebrates black women's contributions.

I remind black women that their aspirations are both valid and achievable.

I radiate positive energy, influencing those around me with good vibes.

I am a beacon of hope, inspiring optimism and confidence.

I freely share my thoughts and feelings, engaging in authentic self-expression.

I offer support with uplifting words, boosting the spirits of those around me.

I am committed to achieving my goals with tenacity and determination.

I foster deep, meaningful connections, enriching my life and those of others.

I bring joy and laughter into my life, creating a light-hearted atmosphere.

I reinforce my belief in my capabilities with positive affirmations.

I face adversity with a strong and resilient spirit, demonstrating my inner strength.

I continuously seek to improve myself, embracing change and growth.

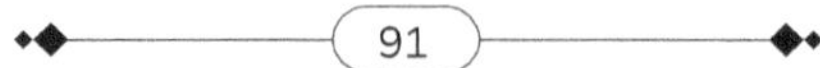

I honor and protect my well-being, setting boundaries that safeguard my peace.

I find balance in my life, managing work, resting, and playing harmoniously.

I appreciate every moment, finding beauty in life's challenges and triumphs.

I maintain a hopeful and positive mindset, focusing on optimistic outcomes.

I confidently showcase my unique qualities and am proud of who I am.

I recognize and celebrate my achievements, acknowledging my progress and successes.

I wisely use my time, engaging in activities that bring joy and fulfillment.

I recover from challenges with increased strength and resilience, ready for what comes next.

I welcome prosperity, embracing abundance in various forms.

I inspire creativity and innovation, fostering a dynamic environment.

I motivate others to follow their dreams, offering encouragement and guidance.

I seek wisdom from every experience, growing more insightful with each lesson.

I practice self-compassion, treating myself with gentleness during challenging times.

I nurture my dreams with commitment and belief, fueling them with passion and energy.

I foster peace within, cultivating tranquility in my surroundings.

I attract good vibes effortlessly, ensuring a positive energy flow in my life.

I demonstrate strength in facing challenges, embodying resilience and courage.

I make clear, value-aligned decisions, ensuring they serve my best interests.

I champion unconditional self-love, embracing every aspect of myself.

I find joy in life's journey, celebrating each step along the way.

I prioritize my well-being, treating self-care as essential.

Success, love, and happiness naturally gravitate towards me, enhancing my daily experience.

My journey inspires others, offering a model of resilience and determination.

I express my unique beauty confidently, appreciating the diversity of my attributes.

Success comes naturally to me, aligning with my actions and intentions.

I claim my destiny as a powerful creator, shaping my future with intention and purpose.

Abundance is my natural state, and I embrace it wholeheartedly.

I embody positivity, radiating light and warmth.

Confidence is second nature, reflected in every aspect of my life.

I am resilient; no challenge is too great for me.

My life's journey showcases my strength and determination.

Prosperity touches all areas of my life, manifesting in varied and fulfilling ways.

Love and joy envelop me, enhancing my interactions and experiences.

Self-love underpins my well-being, grounding me in appreciation for myself.

I welcome the abundance life offers, open to its myriad blessings.

Wealth and success come quickly to me, reflecting my efforts and intentions.

My presence uplifts any space, infusing it with positivity and hope.

Every step is a step towards greatness, moving me closer to my goals.

I radiate confidence, self-assurance, and grace, influencing others with my poise.

I celebrate the magic within me, recognizing the unique gifts I possess.

Success and wellspring are inherently drawn to me, aligning with my vibrational energy.

My mind attracts positive thoughts, creating a magnet for optimism and success.

I release self-doubt, fully embracing my capabilities and power.

I am a beacon of love and kindness, guiding others with empathy and care.

I deserve all the good things life offers, appreciating each blessing that comes my way.

My happiness is within my control, crafted by my choices and perspective.

I trust in my capabilities to attain my goals and am confident in my path to success.

I am a masterpiece, continually evolving and growing in beauty and complexity.

My life is filled with love, joy, and abundance, reflecting the richness of my experiences.

I am surrounded by supporting and encouraging individuals, enhancing my journey.

I am a force for positive change, making impactful contributions to the world.

Success naturally follows my endeavors, aligning with my actions and aspirations.

∞>—•—◇—•—<∞

My heart is open to both giving and receiving love, enriching my emotional well-being.

∞>—•—◇—•—<∞

I am defined by resilience and power, overcoming challenges with strength and grace.

∞>—•—◇—•—<∞

My potential is limitless, offering endless opportunities for growth and achievement.

∞>—•—◇—•—<∞

Others find inspiration in my journey, motivated by my resolve and accomplishments.

∞>—•—◇—•—<∞

I take pride in who I am becoming, recognizing my growth and the impact of my choices.

∞>—•—◇—•—<∞

Confidence and grace accompany me in all situations, shaping my interactions and experiences.

∞>—•—◇—•—<∞

Success and prosperity flow through me, reflecting my alignment with abundance.

I attract positive thoughts, maintaining a mindset that supports my well-being and aspirations.

I confidently shape my destiny, actively creating the life I desire.

Love, success, and happiness are my constant companions, enriching my experiences and interactions.

I cherish my unique traits, understanding they contribute to my particular identity.

My confidence strengthens daily, bolstered by my achievements and self-recognition.

Abundance naturally seeks me out, drawn to my positive energy and successful endeavors.

I fully deserve life's abundant blessings, welcoming them with open arms.

I trust life's journey, even when its direction seems uncertain, knowing that each step is meaningful.

My spirit is indestructible, fortified by resilience and a deep well of inner strength.

Positivity is drawn to me, reflecting my optimistic outlook and vibrant energy.

I effortlessly attract miracles, recognizing the extraordinary in the ordinary.

I release all doubts, fully embracing my authentic self and its boundless potential.

Success is my natural state, achieved through dedication and alignment with my goals.

I inspire others to pursue their dreams, offering guidance and support along the way.

Love and abundance envelop me, creating a life filled with deep satisfaction and joy.

My ability to achieve my goals is unwavering, fueled by determination and clarity.

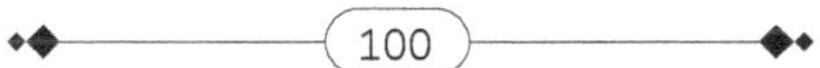

My heart embraces giving and receiving love, fostering rich and fulfilling relationships.

I am a beacon of light, spreading positivity and hope wherever I go.

I rightfully deserve success and all its rewards, recognizing my efforts and their impact.

Each challenge is an opportunity for significant growth and valuable lessons to be learned along the way.

I actively create my reality, shaping my life with intention and vision.

I attract like-minded individuals, building connections that enhance my growth and happiness.

My self-love empowers me to create a fulfilling life rooted in genuine appreciation for myself.

I am resilient and capable of overcoming any challenge with fortitude and wisdom.

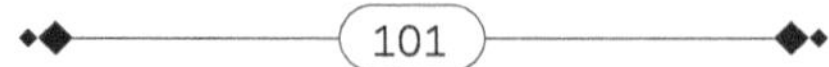

I am grateful for the abundance flowing into my life, recognizing the richness of my blessings.

I am the author of my success story, crafting a narrative filled with achievement and satisfaction.

My life is a masterpiece in progress, beautifully unfolding with each new experience.

I attract opportunities that resonate with my goals, aligning my path with success and fulfillment.

I am a beacon of love and positivity, influencing those around me with warmth and kindness.

I contribute to a compassionate world, actively creating positive change.

I achieve my goals with unwavering determination and focus, attracting success.

I express myself without reservation, serving as a beacon of authenticity.

I empower others, helping them recognize and embrace their inherent strength.

I handle challenges with grace and tenacity, embodying resilience.

I am thankful for the abundance in my life and continuously express gratitude.

I advocate for self-expression, using my voice to challenge stereotypes and uplift black women's diverse narratives.

I promote equality and advocate for black women's representation in all areas of life, acting as a vessel of empowerment.

I inspire others, lighting the path forward with hope and encouragement.

I draw joy and prosperity into my life, becoming a magnet for positive vibrations.

I support black women in expressing their creativity freely, guarding their right to self-expression.

I foster a deep sense of pride and love for our diverse black heritage, creating cultural pride.

I remind black women of the power of their voices and the importance of being heard.

I embrace the journey of self-discovery, championing self-awareness and personal growth.

I uplift others with kindness and compassion, spreading empowerment.

I inspire black women to lead confidently and resiliently, shining as a beacon of inspiration.

I embrace each day with a heart full of courage.

My contributions are recognized and appreciated.

I am the narrator of my own life story.

I thrive under pressure and transform challenges into opportunities.

I am a conduit for inspiration and empowerment.

My inner beauty shines brightly, illuminating the world around me.

I am grounded in the wisdom of my ancestors.

My voice matters, and my words carry weight.

I am in perfect harmony with my surroundings.

I am a pillar of strength and stability for my community.

I define success on my terms.

I attract loving and supportive relationships.

I am a creator of peace and an ambassador of goodwill.

Every decision I make leads me closer to my divine purpose.

I am an agent of change in my community.

My laughter heals my heart and delights my soul.

I deserve a prosperous and fulfilling life.

I honor my needs and prioritize self-care.

My life reflects the love and peace within me.

I am a beacon of creativity and innovation.

My courage transcends fear and inspires others.

I am a living embodiment of grace and resilience.

I recognize and celebrate my growth and achievements.

I am a sacred vessel of love and light.

My actions create constant prosperity.

I am empowered by my experiences and learn from them.

I possess an infinite capacity for love and compassion.

I radiate confidence, and others respect my authority.

My spirit is fortified with joy and a zest for life.

I welcome abundance in all its forms into my life.

I make meaningful contributions to my field and am valued for them.

I am centered, peaceful, and grounded.

My life is full of magical moments.

I am the master of resilience, bending but never breaking.

I spread love and positivity wherever I go.

I honor my intuition and trust my inner guide.

I am connected to a rich heritage of triumph and resilience.

My presence is a source of comfort and joy to others.

I am deserving of love that is abundant, healthy, and fulfilling.

I am the architect of my happiness and build it with grace.

Every cell in my body vibrates with energy and health.

I am a magnet for divine wealth and abundance.

I navigate my journey with faith and confidence.

My life is a beautiful collection of rich experiences.

I am empowered to overcome any obstacle.

I attract success by being my authentic self.

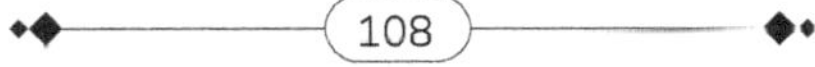

I am committed to living a life of creativity and passion.

I deserve and receive massive amounts of love every day.

My dreams manifest into reality before my eyes.

I am a champion of sisterhood and solidarity.

I choose to thrive in wellness and good health.

I am a joyful celebration of black womanhood.

My mind is clear, focused, and sharp.

I walk in power and speak with confidence.

I am a vibrant channel of peace and tranquility.

My path is carved towards greatness.

I am a curator of inspiration and a motivator for others.

I have a heart full of gratitude and a life full of blessings.

I confidently embrace every part of my journey.

I am a visionary, seeing opportunities where others see obstacles.

I am fierce in my convictions and gentle in my approach.

I am blessed with an incredible family and wonderful friends.

My life is guided by love and driven by purpose.

I possess the wisdom to navigate any situation.

I am a reflection of my ancestors' dreams and achievements.

I am loved for who I am, completely and unconditionally.

I am an infinite being with infinite potential.

I live a life of balance and harmony.

I am connected with the energy of the universe.

My possibilities are endless, and my potential is limitless.

I am a queen crowned in my curls.

My skin is a flawless tapestry of history.

I embrace my unique beauty with pride.

I am worthy of respect and admiration.

My voice is powerful and full of wisdom.

I radiate confidence and grace.

I am a reservoir of strength and resilience.

My heart is brave and bold.

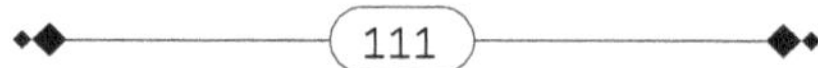

I am deserving of all good things.

My dreams are valid and achievable.

I attract opportunities that help me grow.

I am a beacon of love and warmth.

My potential is limitless.

I am rooted in the beauty of my heritage.

I celebrate my identity every day.

I am equipped to overcome any challenge.

My mind is rich with creative ideas.

I choose to rise above negativity.

I am a powerhouse of innovation and ingenuity.

I am a trailblazer and a trendsetter.

I honor my ancestors through my actions.

I am surrounded by a universe that supports me.

I am healthy, whole, and thriving.

I find joy in my journey.

My spirit is serene and filled with peace.

I trust my intuition and wisdom.

I inspire those around me with my presence.

My life reflects the love I give.

I am financially abundant and secure.

I welcome new adventures with open arms.

I am in charge of my happiness.

I forgive myself and learn from my mistakes.

I am patient and compassionate with myself.

Every day, I grow more into my greatness.

I am a magnet for miracles.

My life is full of beauty and abundance.

I am a leader in my community.

My words are kind and uplifting.

I respect my boundaries and honor my needs.

I am a divine expression of life.

I am loved beyond measure.

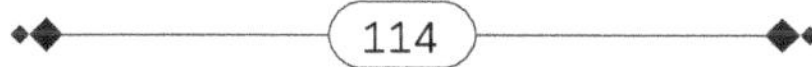

I am proud of my progress.

I choose faith over fear.

I am a symbol of love and devotion.

I am in harmony with the universe.

I am a vessel of peace and calm.

My contributions to the world are valuable.

I am a living legacy of courage and love.

My mind is filled with positive thoughts.

I am the architect of my life's design.

I celebrate my inner and outer beauty.

I am confident in my abilities.

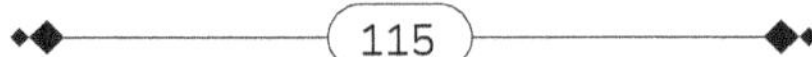

I cherish my spirit of generosity.

I can achieve my highest goals.

I am a positive influence on my community.

My life is rich with positivity and joy.

I embody dignity and poise.

I am a source of wisdom and strength.

I am a warrior dressed in armor of skin.

My laughter is a symphony of joy.

I am a goddess in human form.

I am free to create the life I desire.

My presence is a gift to the world.

I am grateful for my unique talents.

My own hands craft my happiness.

I embrace all cycles of life.

I am a testament to resilience and perseverance.

I am blessed with an abundance of love.

I am a beacon of hope and light.

My journey inspires and motivates.

I am connected to an endless source of creativity.

I am influential and respected.

My words heal, uplift, and empower.

I am committed to personal growth and development.

I radiate beauty, strength, and grace.

My life is a series of wonderful opportunities.

I am a positive force in the universe.

I choose to see the best in people.

I am in control of my destiny.

I treat myself with kindness and love.

I am at peace with my past.

I am excited about what the future holds.

My soul is nourished with love and joy.

I am a beloved child of the universe.

My body is healthy, my mind is brilliant, and my soul is tranquil.

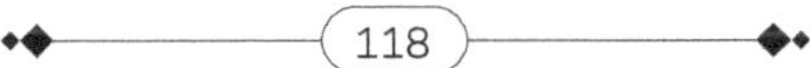

I believe in my abilities and express my true self with ease.

I am unstoppable, resilient, and divinely guided.

I am committed to living a life of integrity and authenticity.

My life is abundant in wealth, health, and happiness.

My spirit is light; I am at peace with myself.

I manifest my reality with thoughtfulness and intention.

I accept and embrace all experiences, even unpleasant ones.

I am constantly growing and evolving into the best version of myself.

I hold the keys to my happiness.

I am deserving of love, peace, and joy.

I am the master of my fate and the captain of my destiny.

My inner world creates my outer world.

Every day, I discover interesting and exciting new paths to pursue.

I trust my journey; I trust the process of life.

Conclusion

As you end this collection of 1020 Positive Daily Affirmations for Black Women, remember that each affirmation is a seed planted in the productive soil of your mind, heart, and spirit. These affirmations are more than words—they are tools for transformation designed to cultivate happiness, health, achievement, confidence, and self-love in your daily life.

Embrace these affirmations as daily companions on your personal growth and empowerment journey. Whether you recite them during your morning routine, reflect on them during a quiet moment, or use them to rise above challenges, let these words resonate deeply, reaffirming your worth and power.

Share these affirmations with friends, family, and anyone in your community who might benefit from a boost of encouragement and strength. Together, you can foster a culture of positivity and support, amplifying the impact of these empowering messages.

As you continue to use these affirmations, watch as your self-esteem strengthens, your resilience grows, and your life reflects the profound truths these statements embody. Remember, you are significant, valued, and incredibly powerful. Let these affirmations be your guide and witness as they help you unfold a life filled with purpose, love, and fulfillment.

Thank you for allowing these affirmations to be a part of your journey.

Continue to shine brightly, inspire others, and embrace each day with courage and joy. You are not just surviving; you are thriving, and each day is a new opportunity to celebrate the incredible woman you are.

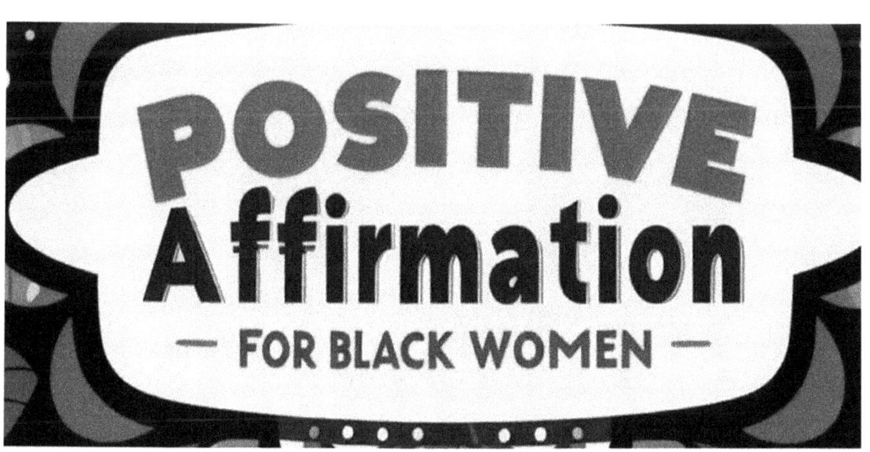